ily! (i love you!)

Gage | 2

A Mother Daughter Relationship Workbook

ily!

(i love you!)

Mother Daughter Relationship Workbook

ily! (i love you!)

Gage | 4

A Mother Daughter Relationship Workbook

ily!

(i love you!) Mother Daughter Relationship Workbook

By

Onedia N. Gage, Ph. D.

ily! (i love you!)

Gage | 6

Other Books by Minister Onedia N. Gage

Are You Ready for 9th Grade . . . Again? A Family's Guide to Success

As We Grow Together Daily Devotional for Expectant Couples

As We Grow Together Prayer Journal for Expectant Couples

The Best 40 Days of Your Life: A Journey of Spiritual Renewal

The Blue Print: Poetry for the Soul

From Two to One: The Notebook for the Christian Couple

Her Story: Bible Study

Her Story: Daily Devotional

Her Story: The Legacy of Her Fight

Her Story: The Legacy Journal

Her Story: Prayers and Journal

In Her Own Words: Notebook for the Christian Woman

In Purple Ink: Poetry for the Spirit

The Intensive Retreat for Couples: Her Workbook

The Intensive Retreat for Couples: His Workbook

Living a Whole Life: Sermons which Prompt, Provoke, and Promote Life

Love Letters to God from a Teenage Girl

The Measure of a Woman: The Details of Her Soul

The Notebook: For Me, About Me, By Me

The Notebook for the Christian Teen

On This Journey Daily Devotional for Young People

On This Journey Prayer Journal for Young People

One Day More Than We Deserve Daily Devotional for the Growing Christian

One Day More Than We Deserve Prayer Journal for the Growing Christian

Promises, Promises: A Christian Novel

Tools for These Times: Timely Sermons for Uncertain Times

With An Anointed Voice: The Power of Prayer

Yielded and Submitted: A Woman's Journey for a Life Dedicated to God

Yielded and Submitted: A Woman's Journey for a Life Dedicated to God Intimate Study

Yielded and Submitted: A Woman's Journey for a Life Dedicated to God Prayers and Journal

ily! (i love you!)

Library of Congress

ily!

(I love you!)

Mother Daughter Relationship Workbook

All Rights Reserved © 2015

Onedia N. Gage

No part of this of book may be reproduced or transmitted in
Any form or by any means, graphic, electronic, or mechanical,
Including photocopying, recording, taping, or by any
Information storage or retrieval system, without the
Permission in writing from the publisher.

Purple Ink, Inc. Press

For Information address:
Purple Ink, Inc
P O Box 300113
Houston, TX 77230
www.purpleink.net
www.onediagage.com

ISBN:

978-1-939119-54-4

Printed in the United States

Dedication

To my daughter

Hillary

God gifted us with each other and

I am truly Grateful.

In this life,

There are defining moments.

Your life is one such defining moment for

Me.

Love,

The Mommy.

To the mothers and daughters who will be healed and enhanced from this workshop and book.

To my new Mothers who pour into my life with a unlimited carafe of knowledge and wisdom.

Thank you for not letting me walk this Earth alone!

ily! (i love you!)

Gage | 10

Dear Mom,

I am truly appreciative that you have taken steps towards enhancing the best human love relationship ever: a mother and her child, and specifically her daughter.

I am excited that you have chosen to study this relationship and take some steps to help the relationship grow.

Mom is also matriarch, who by definition is a woman who rules or dominates a family, group or state. Your job as matriarch is to set the tone for you family, to establish guidelines and boundaries, to establish and honor family traditions and customs. You are designed to have answers. You are the conflict resolver and manager. You are the source of wisdom. You are the secret keeper. You are the mediator. You are the protector. You set the "bar." You orchestrate the direction of your family. You influence decisions that could easily last a century for children you will never meet. You are MOM.

After all of that you may have considered quitting. There is so much more to Mom than putting bows in her hair and buying frilly dresses.

We are to be the most powerful woman in her life. We have to use that power correctly and wisely. Timing is critical.

We are not to be manipulators and con-artists. We are to be encouragers and problem solvers.

In order to do that, we need to be able to do things for ourselves as well. We are only able to do for them what we can do for ourselves.

They are looking to us for these characteristics and information. They need our guidance. We experience several shifts in this relationship. While we are always the parent, the role shifts from overseer to counselor to advisor to consultant. They may ask but may not use your advice. That has to be okay. If you have fostered independent thoughts and out of the box thinking, and ultimately behavior, then you need to consider your "safe" answer/proposal may only be heard.

ily! (i love you!)

You will see yourself differently after this course of study. You will need to consider that carefully. You will hear what she needs. You need to be prepared to respond to those needs. You need to be prepared to hear her real feelings, which is often quite opposite and surprisingly different from what you expected.

Keep your heart, mind and soul open to join with hers. You may have been through the most difficult of times but there is hope that if you keep trying then you can reach a working relationship.

Your goals for her may not look like hers but you can relax in that she will replay conversations with you countless times as she makes life-changing decisions. She does hear you. Be grateful that she has the courage to take risks in front of you. You are there to witness the outcome and you can learn those lessons together. So don't be afraid or angry when she does that, instead embrace her, share with her and applaud her.

Start being courageous as well. Take some risks too. She will respect your courage. If the fact that she takes risks and you don't has ever been an issue, then that friction will reduce because you have shown her that you do not consider courage a bad thing. This is important because she does not want to be judged based on her courage or her perception of your lack thereof.

Please share you story with me at any time. I can be contacted at onediagage@purpleink.net, @onediangage (twitter), and facebook.com/onediagage. You can view my materials on youtube.com/onediagage and listen to my radio shows on blogtalkradio.com/onediagage.

Let's roll.

I'm mommy,

Onedia N. Gage

Dear Daughter,

Greetings! I am encouraged that you are holding this workbook. It means that you are invested in the relationship with your mother and are willing to invest more. It speaks volumes that you are present in that relationship. It means that you desire and maybe even demand that you all have a relationship.

Maybe you recognize the power of a great mother/daughter relationship or you simply envy what you see with other mother/daughters. Whatever your reason, just know that I am excited for you in this endeavor. The relationship is worth it. It is valuable. It is powerful.

You are valuable. You are powerful because of it. This relationship offers you freedom and wisdom. That means that you have the full benefit of her experience and wisdom to live this life on your own. New options plus conventional wisdom is a powerful combination. There is an idiom which says, "If I knew then, what I know now, I would be so much better off." In your situation, you have the benefit of what she knows now based on then coupled with what you know now, you could avoid so many mistakes. You should only pay for half of your own mistakes because you only have to make half. Your mother should be able, allowed, invited to share in your life at a level where you should not make as many mistakes.

Be patient with your mother regarding transparency. This is a new place for most parents. We did not grow up with it and now that you are demanding it, we are scared. You are asking your mother to reveal her secrets and possibly embarrassing moments in order to equip you with a better life. Sometimes she would rather die. She does not want to lose your respect or to be judged by you because she did something silly as a teenager and young adult.

Your mother is not your friend. She is your mother. She cannot sacrifice that role by trying to be your friend. You will have hundreds, even thousands in your lifetime. She will not be one. There is a huge difference. You should not reduce her to a friend and she should resist every urge and desire to do so as well.

She is a remarkably powerful woman. Her charge is to equip you to be the same. Listening is required of you to help the success of that. I need you to understand that you are the daughter. You are being trained and molded to withstand the pressures and demands of this world. She has/had exactly 6,574 days to

ily! (i love you!)

accomplish this goal. That is 18 years. Inside of that 18 years, she has to be prepared to give you to the college of your choice, the military, or a career. She has to do a great job or you will arrive in the middle of nowhere feeling lost and helpless and wanting to come home. Stay focused on being prepared. You are more likely to succeed in your endeavors if you feel prepared.

You are her report card. She wants an A but that grade is earned based on your life and its changes. If you flunk out of college, or go AWOL in the military or if you become a criminal or become addicted to drugs, chances are she will grade herself with an F.

When you do something wrong or inappropriate the first thing people say is 'didn't your mother teach you anything.' Your response needs to be, 'she tried but I wasn't paying attention.' They have judged her not you.

Your mother is critical in your life. She deserves your respect. REGARDLESS.

Be a great daughter. Be fearless. Be courageous. Be loving. Be smart. Be kind. Be respectful. Be honest. Be her daughter.

I look forward to hearing how you have grown from this workbook. I can be reached on Instagram—Ongage, twitter @onediangage, facebook.com/onediagage, youtube.com/onediagage, blogtalkradio.com/onediagage, or via email onediagage@onediagage.com or onediagage@purpleink.net

I am a daughter too,

Onedia Gage

Table of Contents

Dedication	9
Letter to Mom	11
Letter to Daughter	13
Instructions for Use	17
Definitions	19
Objectives and Goals	21
Mother/Daughter Contract	23
Mother/Daughter Covenant	24
Love	27
Roles	43
Communication	51
Expectations	63
Truth	73
Consequences of Great and Poor Relationships	83
Legacy	91
Technology	103

ily! (i love you!)

Quality Time	113
Transparency	125
ILY! Conclusion	135
Appendix	139
Calendars blank	140
Ideas for activities	142
All About Me Quiz	143
Suggested Questions	145
Plan for Conflict Resolution	146
Goals Worksheet	147
Mission Worksheet	149
Vision Worksheet	150
Value Worksheet	151
Dreams Worksheet	152
Resources	153
Acknowledgements	155
About the Mother/Daughter/Author/ Facilitator	157

Instructions for Use

This workbook is a living document. You will read and write in this workbook.

Here are the rules:

1. Be honest.
2. Be transparent.
3. Be open.
4. Be forgiving.
5. Be loving.
6. Be expecting a break through.
7. Be authentic.
8. Be assertive.
9. Be respectful.
10. Be judicious.
11. Be ready to learn.
12. Be ready to succeed.
13. Be ready to be loved.
14. Be thankful.
15. Be resourceful.
16. Be persistent.
17. Be diligent.
18. Be hopeful.
19. Be optimistic.
20. Be courageous.

You will share some of you stuff but remain clam. The outcome is important, more important than almost everything else.

Maintain respect even if angry. Answer all that you can. If you cannot, come back to it later.

ily! (i love you!)

Gage | 18

Definitions

Mother, n: a female parent; source, origin

Daughter, n: a female offspring

Relationship (relation) n: an aspect or quality (as resemblance) that connects two or more things as parts as being or belonging or working together or as being of the same kind.

ily! (i love you!)

Gage | 20

OBJECTIVES

Objective: to enhance an existing mother/daughter relationship.

Your objective:

_____

_____

_____

_____

_____

_____

Her objective:

_____

_____

_____

_____

_____

ily! (i love you!)

GOALS

What do you want to achieve from this workbook?

_____
_____
_____
_____

How will that be achieved?

_____
_____
_____
_____

Goals   Your Goals   Her Goals

1. To have better communication
2. To have better respect
3. To love more openly, freely
4. To understand her better
5. To listen and respond appropriately
6. To form a stronger bond

Contract: Mother/Daughter

- I will do my best in this workbook, working relationship to make this relationship work.
- I will keep her secrets a secret. I will keep her trust sacred.
- I will not judge her for what she shares and who she is.
- I will support her goals and feed her dreams.
- I will open to hear her and I will listen attentively.
- I will not criticize her thoughts or deeds.
- I will show her what she does not know and help create within her a thirst for learning and the positive atmosphere to be successful.
- I will keep my word, my promises.
- I will be honest and trustworthy.
- I will honor our relationship at all levels.
- I will forgive her in real time. I will avoid the temptation and the opportunity to rewind and relish the event which needed forgiveness.
- I will seek to understand her needs without trying to fix everything.
- I will listen to her.
- I am an advocate for her.
- I am a source for her but not all of the answers. I will not be jealous when she seeks information from others.
- I will love without condition.
- I will consider her feelings when I speak, suggesting my experiences.
- I will remember that we are family, assigned by God to be together.
- I will take care of my physical health.

_____   _____
Mom   Daughter

ily! (i love you!)

Mother/Daughter Covenant

I vow to

- Honor you in your role
- Respect your feelings
- Hear you concerns
- Be transparent about my needs
- Love freely
- Forgive
- Share openly
- Be honest in my communication
- Be whole, healthy and wise
- Be conscious of how I make you feel when I share
- Respect the privacy of our conversations
- Respect the privacy of your personal secrets
- Trust you
- Love extravagantly
- Complete this study
- Spend quality time with her each week
- Increase my communication
- Be patient with her as we grow

You will each need to sign the covenant in each book

_____   _____   _____   _____
Mother   Date   Daughter   Date

ily!

(i love you!)

A Mother Daughter Relationship Workbook

ily! (i love you!)

> Motherhood
>
> Is a choice you make everyday
>
> To put someone else's happiness and well-being
>
> ahead of your own.
>
> To teach the hard lessons.
>
> To do the right thing, even when you are
>
> Not sure what the right thing is.
>
> And to forgive yourself over and over again for doing
>
> Everything wrong.
>
> —Anonymous

Love

Love is a verb. It is graded based on action. We all define what that looks like differently but we can agree that it is based on what you do. Some people, especially children, equate love with time. The more time you spend, the more you love. While that may not be the case when you spend less time, you do not love, it's the recipient's perception that matters the most.

ILY! is how this started. There was a class of young ladies and their mothers. The discussion was on text messaging and text language. One mom blurted out, "What does ily mean?" Before the teacher's answer could be offered, the daughter burst out, "I love you!" The mom blushed with embarrassment and was equally excited. The daughter seemed broken. What took place next was the ah-ha moment, the break through. "So you didn't know what that meant so you hadn't responded?" The mother responded ashamedly, "No. I didn't know. No, I didn't ask." "So did you think that Mom did not love you because she did not respond?" "Yes, I did not think so." "Did it ever occur to you that she did not know what it meant? Further, did you ever introduce the acronym?" "Not at all," Mom apologized and they hugged.

How long were they going to have that unknown misunderstanding?

People receive and interpret love differently. Some have to see it. Others have to touch it. Still others have to hear it. Some of us need to have it two ways. However you perceive love, and however we receive love, it is essential to receive love. It is essential to give love.

Love and the amount in our love tank is essential for how we live, love and respond. Your love tank, from Gary Chapman's <u>Five Love Languages</u>, is the reservoir where love deposits are stored. As those deposits are made, you feel more loved. When deposits are not made, the less love you feel.

Love is shared in many ways. First of all, mothers love their daughters just because you are here. There is NOTHING you can do that will increase her love for you. Every circumstance maybe different, however overall, a mother loves her daughter…….unconditionally.

We define love differently. We demonstrate love differently. We are dedicated to love differently. As we learn each other's love style, we can use what we know to grow toward each other. Sharing your personal definition of love is critical to her understanding your love style and how it compares to yours.

ily! (i love you!)

Likewise how it differs from yours. This knowledge is designed to understand how to meet her needs for love.

Remember the definition will evolve and develop. When you notice a change within yourself, it is fair and customary to announce that change or addition. She is not a mind reader and neither are you. She is not a heart reader and neither are you. Share when you have additional love definitions or expectations.

Your demonstration is also quite unique to you. As you age and mature, that demonstration changes. Few events are more disturbing than your daughter no longer wants to be hugged just because she is older now. With our demonstration of love, we should exercise some sensitivity to her needs. If she needs to be hugged but you would prefer to be swallowed whole by a bear, then you should figure out how to hug her and not die. She is related to you. She loves you! Do consider the fact that if you do not love her the way she receives it best, she will not feel loved, and she will act unloving. This unloving behavior produces other behavior that is also inappropriate. Love and be loved!

As we dedicate ourselves to love, we are reminded that we are not perfect so we will make some mistakes. Love is forgiving. Love is an exercise of forgiveness. Love is an exhibit of forgiving. Dedication to love sometimes means we need a re-start or a do-over. Love means going the extra distance, which is often further that the extra mile.

As you define and possibly redefine love, please be conscious of sharing that definition. You unconsciously hold her accountable for that definition but she does not know what that definition is nor how to function effectively with it.

There is a story entitles Guess How Much I Love You by Sam McBratney, about a father rabbit and a son rabbit. In this dialogue between the two, they are comparing how much they love each other. For every point the baby makes, the father surpasses him. There is one point when the baby says I love you to my toes. At that point, the father swings the baby over his head and says that I live you to my toes which is more that's because of their height difference.

The point the father makes is that as my child, you cannot love me more than I love you. No matter what you do.

We each have the right to assume we love more. Our goal is to be loving and be loved at all times. Love is not optional.

How do you define love? How do you share that definition of love? What happens when the other person does not feel loved by you? This is the crossroads that most mother/daughter teams made at some point.

How do we communicate our love to one another? How do we love when we don't want to? How do we help the other one to be more lovable?

Love is essential and critical for the emotional stability and growth of each other. Do we handle the other person like we love each other?

ily! (i love you!)

MOTHER/DAUGHTER ANECDOTE: LOVE

I experienced love at first sight with my daughter. The love that a mother should have for a daughter is indescribable!

Our afternoon we were playing together. She accomplished something. She announced her accomplishment. I did not respond immediately, so she said, "Mommy, put your pen down and clap for me!" She was three years old. She surprised me by saying that. I certainly did what she said: I put my pen down and clapped for her.

I learned that my daughter's love language was words of affirmation—praise and encouragement. I then understood that in order for her to know that I loved her, I had to use my words to encourage her even when I disciplined her. I am thankful that I am gifted with words so I was not struggling to know what to say to her to lift her countenance.

I still show her love by writing her notes, sending texts, emails and cards. I cheer as loud as I can when she plays basketball. She knows my voice and lights up with a smile when she hears my voice. It is important that she understands that I love her. My love needs to override the outside voices. My love overpowers the struggle of self-identity and any identity crisis.

My love has to sustain her through storms, pain, and trauma. My voice has to override the idea of suicide, wrongdoings, and any other issue. My love has to lift her head when she is down, bordering on depression, and when the view seems hopeless. My love has to override the internal voice of self-doubt, and the fear that may seep into her heart. My love has to agree with her when she is confident and zealous, proud and ecstatic. My love has to encourage her to continue especially when there is a struggle. There is no time for her to doubt my love. A mother's love is the most important. My love has to encourage her to try harder, run faster, believe more, go farther, and achieve all that she desires.

My love has the ability to override, overrule, adjust, and encourage. Every day is critical and each day counts.

I love her every day, especially when I do not see her. My love is powerful! I need to love her freely and openly.

Gage | 30

WRITE HER A LOVE LETTER.

Mothers are writing to daughters. Daughters are writing to mothers.

ily! (i love you!)

Does her love inspire you to love others better? Explain.

_____
_____
_____
_____

Does her love inspire you to love better? Explain.

_____
_____
_____
_____

How does she know that you love her? Be specific.

_____
_____
_____
_____
_____

Does she ever doubt your love? Why?

_____
_____
_____
_____

Has she ever said or done anything that indicates that she does not love you? Explain.

_____
_____
_____
_____

Has she ever said that she does not love you? Explain.

_____
_____
_____
_____

How can you demonstrate love better to her?

_____
_____
_____
_____

ily! (i love you!)

What is your love language? Were you surprised? Explain how you will respond now that you know what your love language is.

_____
_____
_____
_____
_____

What is her love language? Were you surprised? Explain how you will respond now that you know what her love language is.

_____
_____
_____
_____
_____

How do you plan to improve her perception of your love for her?

_____
_____
_____
_____
_____

What do you want her to do so that you will know that she loves you?

_____
_____
_____
_____
_____

Are you confusing love with approval? Or lack thereof? Explain.

_____
_____
_____
_____
_____

How do you define love?

_____
_____
_____
_____
_____

ily! (i love you!)

How does she define love? How did you decide that? Did you ask her?

_____
_____
_____
_____
_____

How far apart are those definitions?

_____
_____
_____
_____
_____

Is it hard to love her? Why?

_____
_____
_____
_____
_____
_____

Is your love for her an example for others? Explain.

_____
_____
_____
_____

Do you love yourself by your own definition? Explain.

_____
_____
_____
_____

How can you increase your love for her?

_____
_____
_____
_____
_____

ily! (i love you!)

How would you like to be loved? How did you arrive at that definition? Have you ever explained that to her or anyone else?

_____
_____
_____
_____
_____

What would I tell her if I didn't have to worry about getting in trouble or ruining the relationship?

_____
_____
_____
_____
_____
_____
_____
_____
_____
_____
_____
_____
_____
_____
_____
_____

ily! (i love you!)

REFLECTION

- What have you learned?
- What will you share about this study with others?
- How will you change based on what you have learned?
- How will you influence/inspire her/others to understand your new behavior/attitude?
- What questions do you still have about her based on this lesson?

_____
_____
_____
_____
_____
_____
_____
_____
_____
_____
_____
_____

RESOURCES

The Five Love Language Quiz   www.5lovelanguages.com/profile/

Love Poems by Nikki Giovanni

I Corinthians 13:1-13, NIV, MSG

13 If I speak with human eloquence and angelic ecstasy but don't love, I'm nothing but the creaking of a rusty gate.

² If I speak God's Word with power, revealing all his mysteries and making everything plain as day, and if I have faith that says to a mountain, "Jump," and it jumps, but I don't love, I'm nothing.

³⁻⁷ If I give everything I own to the poor and even go to the stake to be burned as a martyr, but I don't love, I've gotten nowhere. So, no matter what I say, what I believe, and what I do, I'm bankrupt without love.

Love never gives up.
Love cares more for others than for self.
Love doesn't want what it doesn't have.
Love doesn't strut,
Doesn't have a swelled head,
Doesn't force itself on others,
Isn't always "me first,"
Doesn't fly off the handle,
Doesn't keep score of the sins of others,
Doesn't revel when others grovel,
Takes pleasure in the flowering of truth,
Puts up with anything,
Trusts God always,
Always looks for the best,
Never looks back,
But keeps going to the end.

ily! (i love you!)

⁸⁻¹⁰ Love never dies. Inspired speech will be over some day; praying in tongues will end; understanding will reach its limit. We know only a portion of the truth, and what we say about God is always incomplete. But when the Complete arrives, our incompletes will be canceled.

¹¹ When I was an infant at my mother's breast, I gurgled and cooed like any infant. When I grew up, I left those infant ways for good.

¹² We don't yet see things clearly. We're squinting in a fog, peering through a mist. But it won't be long before the weather clears and the sun shines bright! We'll see it all then, see it all as clearly as God sees us, knowing him directly just as he knows us!

¹³ But for right now, until that completeness, we have three things to do to lead us toward that consummation: Trust steadily in God, hope unswervingly, love extravagantly. And the best of the three is love.

Ephesians 4:32 (NIV)

³² Be kind and compassionate to one another, forgiving each other, just as in Christ God forgave you.

John 3:16 (NIV)

¹⁶ For God so loved the world that He gave His one and only Son, that whoever believes in Him shall not perish but have eternal life.

Roles

Mother- Teach me everything.

Daughter- Clean your room.

What are your roles in this life? What are your roles in this relationship?

There are some definite roles and then there are negotiable roles in this relationship. The role is defined as your job. The role includes what you are responsible for doing. The role includes what you need to accomplish in this role.

Mother

As a mother, we have to complete several tasks regarding our daughters. We are responsible for the overall outcome of our daughters. Share. Teach. Show. Demonstrate. Model. Adapt. Overcome. Manage. Lead. Talk. Listen. Discipline. Advise. Discuss. Deliberate. Debate. Empower. Embrace. Encourage. Enlighten. Believe. Instruct. Peace keeper. Promise keeper. Negotiator. Planner. Coach. Advocate. Search. Seize. Translate. Interpret. Expand. Expound. Extend. Equip. Deliver. Deny. Provide. Participate. Juggle. Transport. Think. Feel. Remind. Promote. Shop. Organize. Work. Mind read. Guess. Host. Invite. Socialize. Wait. Analyze. Network. Research. Duplicate. Learn. Create. Creative. Positive. Initiative. Intuition. Warning. Loving.

All of these words are part of our job description. Moms are a comprehensive being that has to rise to many occasions and situations. These words may not be a complete list. Mothers have to be the total solution. Often at the last minute and under a tight deadline, which may be overwhelming and stressful.

As a parent, we are depended upon for everything the daughter needs. Mothers are mostly responsible for the daughter's appearance in the world.

Mothers grade other mothers on how the children respond and behave. When a child is off-task, the first thing that comes to the mind of the mother present is, "Where is her mother?" "Did she teach you anything?" "Where is the mother right now?"

As the mother, our role is to instruct, direct, and repeat until what we are teaching is in full practice. How does a mother manage that? Mothers have to insure a child's understanding of what the world will throw

ily! (i love you!)

at them. Big task? Absolutely! Further Mothers have personal standards. Those personal standards are created through our personal experiences.

Mothers have an awesome responsibility. These standards distinguish us from those who will be successful in this life and those who will struggle in this life.

Mothers are graded on how much our children know, how well our children behave, how much our children learn, how much our children learn, and how our children respond to others. Mothers have a report card based on the lives of her children. Her work will yield a return. If she does not invest in her child's life, then she will not reap a return on that investment. Mothers are charged with sharing what is supposed to equip you as daughters to manage life. Mothers are supposed to support what she teaches and shares. When our children are successful or if they are failures, mothers are graded. Whether our children are obedient to our lessons or not, mothers are still held accountable.

Further, mothers grade each other severely – maybe more than we should. However, mothers are judged by the success, value, worth and productivity of our children. Regardless of the nature of your efforts, mothers are judged and graded on what our children does with our instruction. The mother should have an extensive influence over the outcome of our children.

Not one mother will ever admit that it will be okay to have a sorry, lazy daughter.

Mother, your job is to teach.

Daughter, your job is to apply what you learn.

Mothers teach:	**Daughters learn:**
Eating	etiquette
Walking	poise
Sleeping	grace
Reading	literacy
Loving	love
Loving	to love

Playing	to have fun
Math	to think

Daughter

One of the statements that mothers make repeatedly is "clean your room!" These are three most hated words to a daughter's ears. However, these are some very important words. When Mom says, "Clean your room," this statement needs to be led by showing you how to clean that room. Cleaning that room teaches you organization, cleanliness, and discipline. These skills will be carried forward for the rest of your life. Daughter, your cleanliness is a report card of your mother's work ethic.

Daughter, as you go to college, the way you keep your room and your belongings reflects on your mother. Your mother will need to walk in your dormitory and future home and be proud of what she sees and smells. We are not discussing decorating. We are speaking of neat drawers, closets, under beds, and completely dust free.

Mother, when you upgrade your lessons, please share your changes with her.

Daughter, please take these lessons to heart. You will soon realize that your lessons are important and the time you have with your mother is not promised and is precious. You will start to meet people who will not have mothers and some will not have the same comprehensive story that you have had.

Clean your room daughter! And do whatever else you need to do so that you will have the tools you need to be a great woman, eventually a mother, which is when most of us reach the level of knowledge we need to understand the previous years.

Daughter, it is often hard to understand why Mother does what she does. However, there are future reasons for her behavior and these activities result in lessons which you will need and will share.

ily! (i love you!)

Daughter—based on what you have seen, how will you behave/respond differently now that you know the extension of the lesson of clean your room?

_____
_____
_____
_____
_____
_____

Mother – will you consider cleaning her room with her so she will KNOW your expectations and appreciate the example of how to meet your expectations?

_____
_____
_____
_____
_____
_____

What would I tell her if I didn't have to worry about getting in trouble or ruining the relationship?

ily! (i love you!)

REFLECTION

- What have you learned?
- What will you share about this study with others?
- How will you change based on what you have learned?
- How will you influence/inspire her/others to understand your new behavior/attitude?
- What questions do you still have about her based on this lesson?

_____
_____
_____
_____
_____
_____
_____
_____
_____
_____
_____
_____

Resources

Psalm 139:13 (NIV)

¹³ For you created my inmost being;
   you knit me together in my mother's womb.

Proverbs 1:8 (NIV)

⁸ Listen, my son, to your father's instruction
   and do not forsake your mother's teaching.

Psalm 71:6 (NIV)

⁶ From birth I have relied on you;
   you brought me forth from my mother's womb.
   I will ever praise you.

Matthew 15:4 (NIV)

⁴ For God said, 'Honor your father and mother' and 'Anyone who curses their father or mother is to be put to death.'

ily! (i love you!)

Communication

Ask	Share
Answer	Ask
Share	Answer
Listen	Listen

Communication is REQUIRED for successful relationships. Communication is defined as the imparting or interchange of thoughts, opinions, or information by speech, writing or signs. Communication between a mother and daughter has to be effective and meaningful. Communication between a mother and daughter needs to be honest and transparent.

There is one essential element that we need to cover with regards to mothers and daughters. Daughter, when you seek or hear the advice of another person, whose advice you also follow, and if your mother has ever told the same information, know that your mother will be offended. The fact that you did what she suggested does not make it right. You should have listened to her the first time. She is your mother. She should be your authority. Under the unfortunate circumstances that Mother is not respected anymore or that she did something which eroded your trust in her, Daughter please give her the respect she deserves. Now, daughter I have many stories about Mothers who have given excellent advice to her daughter but her daughter did not choose to act on that advice until someone else gave that same advice. Do not be that same daughter.

Mother

This has been proven difficult for many. Mom, what should you be communicating about? I'm glad you asked. Half of the time should be spent listening and the other half should be talking. The talking should be split between sharing wisdom and asking questions. When sharing, we are to share information she needs for the rest of her life, what she needs to pass on to your grandchildren, and help for healthy living.

ily! (i love you!)

Share everything that you wished your mother had told you. Share everything that you needed to know. Share the unique and the extraordinary. Share the taboo and unthinkable. Share boldly. Share wisely. Share family anecdotes and history. Sharing makes you wise, Mom. Sharing requires meekness and humility and transparency. Sharing allows her to trust. Sharing compels her to believe. Sharing reminds her of credibility. Sharing equips her. Sharing stops you from asking why doesn't she act like when she knows better. Sharing insures the she acts better because she knows better.

Not sharing is lying by omission. While that was acceptable when you were the daughter, it will not establish you as the sought after mother. When I say share boldly, I am offering you the opportunity to share the truth about family history, difficult times, health history, and other facts. Most of us do not share because we are too good now and too embarrassed about decisions we made and the hardships we endured. I propose we share to end generational curses.

Sharing dos not change the outcome but if you become vulnerable which gives you the power to influence her and her decisions before you have to "kick" yourself and have to say "I wish I had" when she tells you that she had the VERY experience you hoped she would not.

Daughter

You communicate through body language. Most of that body language is not good. Often it is hostile and closed to hearing what your mother has to say. Your body language stops you from listening and stops you from talking.

Further, the main complaint of mothers is that their daughters have volatile attitudes and an incredibly horrible body language. This may be true. Your body language displays anger and your disposition needs some work.

You are responsible for a percentage of the mother/daughter relationship and communication as much as Mom is. You have to realize that whatever the reason for the organization of the anger and hostility, you are KEY to resuming that much needed relationship. So that translates into you have to forgive and dissolve the attitude and tell of the negative feelings in order to reach that great place.

Communication with your mother is valuable even though she had made it difficult previously. You do have to remember that she is also learning the communication part as well. Mothers communicate with each child differently. So even though she may not be a new mom, her experience only gets her so far with you. Further, consider that you are holding her to an unspoken standard. If you do not share, she will never understand what you want or need.

Communication is more than talking and body language. This includes texting and emails. You are communicating in more means that other mother and daughters have had access to. Mom may not be a texter or emailer or social media guru. Meet her where she is. Help her with some additional mediums.

Find value in the relationship. Use communication to reach that understanding of value. Stop thinking that you will know her response. Stop assuming that her response will be negative. Ask for what you need and want, then wait on her to deliver.

Communication tends to clear up the normal misunderstandings. You are responsible for sharing as well. You have to leave behind the old issues and the past hurts. Sharing requires honesty, transparency, and maturity. Bring your honesty, transparency and maturity to the table. It is the best thing for your relationship.

Further remember you are in rehearsal to be a mom as well. Practice being the Mom that you want your child to experience.

ily! (i love you!)

Communication Anecdote

I love to talk, however, my mother does not. I thought it was my fault, however it is not my fault that she does not like to talk, nor that she does not like to talk to me.

This does not make for healthy, happy or whole. When a child has to seek someone else a listening ear, it will often not be someone we would have selected or recommended. But by then it is too late because you already rejected her.

My daughter realized that I love to talk but I like her voice as well. I encourage her to talk, explain and otherwise, hear her own voice. This becomes valuable since she needs to hear what she sounds like.

She mostly talks about school and sports (basketball) so I listen intently and recognize when she needs my guidance and leadership.

Effective communication is bred. This is not an innate skill or something someone else does.

I am doing for her what was not done for me.

When your baby was born, you did not understand anything she said but with much effort on both parts, you were finally able to recognize her words. You simply didn't speak the same language yet.

As she grew, her vocabulary expanded and the communication got much better.

Now as a teenager, we are subject to not understand her again. Our mutual understanding requires mutual effort.

In order to survive this season and move into the adulthood we so anxiously anticipate, we must work to understand each other.

What should you be saying that you are not? Explain.

_____
_____
_____
_____

Why aren't you listening to her? Explain.

_____
_____
_____
_____

Why isn't she listening to you? Explain. Give specific examples.

_____
_____
_____
_____

ily! (i love you!)

What is the reason you cannot communicate effectively? Explain.
_____
_____
_____
_____
_____

What would help your communication?
_____
_____
_____
_____

Do you need help with what to talk about? Explain. Why?
_____
_____
_____

Do you need a translator for what she is saying? How are you going to achieve that?
_____
_____

Do you need help with your tone when speaking to her? Explain.

_____
_____
_____

Do you need to pray before you speak? Explain.

_____
_____
_____

Do you have trouble asking her for clarity in what she says? Explain.

_____
_____
_____

Do you have a mediator who could assist with helping you to articulate what you need to say to her? That person would also keep the conversation healthy and progressing.

_____
_____
_____
_____

ily! (i love you!)

What would I tell her if I didn't have to worry about getting in trouble or ruining the relationship?

REFLECTION

- What have you learned?
- What will you share about this study with others?
- How will you change based on what you have learned?
- How will you influence/inspire her/others to understand your new behavior/attitude?
- What questions do you still have about her based on this lesson?

_____

_____

_____

_____

_____

_____

_____

_____

_____

_____

_____

ily! (i love you!)

RESOURCES

Psalm 19:14

¹⁴ May these words of my mouth and this meditation of my heart
    be pleasing in your sight, LORD, my Rock and my Redeemer.

Proverbs 10:31

³¹ From the mouth of the righteous comes the fruit of wisdom, but a perverse tongue will be silenced.

Proverbs 15:4

⁴ The soothing tongue is a tree of life, but a perverse tongue crushes the spirit.

Psalm 34:13

¹³ keep your tongue from evil and your lips from telling lies.

Proverbs 16:1

To humans belong the plans of the heart, but from the LORD comes the proper answer of the tongue.

Matthew 12:34

³⁴ You brood of vipers, how can you who are evil say anything good? For the mouth speaks what the heart is full of.

Psalm 37:30

³⁰ The mouths of the righteous utter wisdom, and their tongues speak what is just.

Proverbs 18:2

² Fools find no pleasure in understanding, but delight in airing their own opinions.

Matthew 15:11

[11] What goes into someone's mouth does not defile them, but what comes out of their mouth, that is what defiles them."

Psalm 139:4

[4] Before a word is on my tongue you, LORD, know it completely.

Psalm 39:1

[1] I said, "I will watch my ways and keep my tongue from sin;
I will put a muzzle on my mouth while in the presence of the wicked."

2 Samuel 23:2

[2] "The Spirit of the LORD spoke through me; his word was on my tongue.

Proverbs 15:2

[2] The tongue of the wise adorns knowledge, but the mouth of the fool gushes folly.

Job 34:3

[3] For the ear tests words as the tongue tastes food.

Proverbs 17:20

[20] One whose heart is corrupt does not prosper; one whose tongue is perverse falls into trouble.

Job 15:5

[5] Your sin prompts your mouth; you adopt the tongue of the crafty.

Proverbs 21:23

[23] Those who guard their mouths and their tongues keep themselves from calamity.

ily! (i love you!)

Job 27:4

⁴ my lips will not say anything wicked, and my tongue will not utter lies.

Proverbs 31:26

²⁶ She speaks with wisdom, and faithful instruction is on her tongue.

Job 33:2

² I am about to open my mouth; my words are on the tip of my tongue.

Isaiah 32:4

⁴ The fearful heart will know and understand,
 and the stammering tongue will be fluent and clear.

Expectations

What should you expect from your daughter?

What should you expect from your mother?

Your family is a brand. There are numerous examples when someone has asked you if you know someone because you share a last name with someone they know. When that question is asked you do not ever know if it is good or bad. Invariably, it is a question of "are you related."

Do you want to be the mother she is embarrassed about? Do you want to be the daughter she is ashamed of? The answer is no. The answer is no.

Expectations dictate that we meet each other's expectations in every aspect of life. Will some of them seem overwhelming? Absolutely! However, we can meet them with an open heart if we are willing to meet them.

Mother

Mom, what do you expect of her? If there were a list, it may read: earn good grades, respectful, obedient, great work ethic, a clean room and a whole healthy and happy soul. Please add good character and good reputation. While these are great and reasonable, we need to consider how we share those expectations, along with how those expectations were established and why they are important expectations.

When you develop the expectations and structure the expectations, how do you share this information? Do you let her help develop the expectations and consequences? Does she participate in the development of the consequences for not meeting these expectations? Does she really understand what these expectations expand into later as a woman? Does she know that she will pass on these expectations to her children? Did you tell her when to use expectations came from?

So my expectations are good grades, healthy attitude, respectful demeanor and tone, and communication. Obedience is obviously one as well.

ily! (i love you!)

I also expect your very best at all times. When her best is not available, then she needs to seek help on how to let her best be present during adversity. I expect my daughter to separate herself from the negative talk, including mine, if ever that happened. She does NOT have to listen to someone who declares what she is incapable of and what she cannot achieve. Those persons are IGNORED.

I expect her to dream and dream big. I expect her to have faith and to hope for the best. I challenge her to remain positive in adversity and be optimistic when chances look bleak.

What are your expectations?

Know in this matter, I want to point out that these children are a new breed of children. You should expect that if you are not a model for what you speak, then you will be challenged and possibly feel disrespected. I am not advocating either however, I am warning you that this is not a "do as I say" generation. That is hard for some of us because we grew up in an opposite generation.

Daughter

Expectations are of considerable importance for you and your mother. Failed expectations are often the reason for poor relationships. The best way to avoid the failed expectations is to annunciate those expectations – clearly, specifically, and repeatedly. This means you, too! You are responsible for sharing the expectations you have of your mother, the source of those expectations and the rationale of the expectations. Keep in mind she has the option to dismiss those expectations, without cause or reason. You, as the daughter will obviously not have any of your expectations met if she does not know what they are.

What are you expecting from your mother?

Where did you gather those expectations from?

What is your rationale for those expectations?

How do you hope to hold her accountable for these expectations?

You are expecting her to be your mom and each of us has a definition of that so prepare to share what being my mom means. Your mother does not know how to be your specific mother. You mother is actually the mother that she wishes she had. She is being the mom that's she thinks is best. She never considered what kind of mom you need.

It is worth whatever it takes to communicate your expectations to her so that you can help insure that you have a healthy relationship with her.

It is fair that whatever you let her guess, assume and continue to do that stifles your relationship, you should continue to suffer through.

You are the daughter that she birthed. She deserves to know that so that you both can be successful.

It is not fair to expect something from someone but never share that expectation. You would not want to be held accountable for something you were unaware of.

ily! (i love you!)

Expectations Anecdote

As a mother, I expect some elements from my daughter and she seems to know the expectations exist. She also knows how to fulfill those expectations. When she has challenges meeting those expectations, she also knows to communicate any possible issues with meeting those expectations. She is also clear about the consequences of not meeting the expectations and not communicating with me about arising issues. On the other hand, I am sure to reward her when she goes above those expectations and I am sure to recognize her when she meets those expectations without my involvement directly. I make sure that I recognize her when that happens.

There is an expectation that my daughter has established with me as well. "Put your pen down and clap for me!" She was three years old when she made that announcement. She caused me to understand how powerful my praise and encouragement of her. From that day to this, I have been able to recognize her in her greatness. Her attitude is great because I recognize her. She expects me to share with her my regard for her actions and activities. She deserves my recognition!

As a daughter, I was not afforded my expectations. I expected love from my mother. I wanted that love exhibited through physical affection, such as hugs and physical proximity. My mother did not hug or let me be close to her, neither physically or emotionally.

This distance that was established diminished the nature of the kind of relationship which nurtures and grows in a healthy manner.

She created a divide between us because the very expectations I had for our relationship were impaired. This is unhealthy for the spirit, but I still survived.

Does your daughter deserve you to quit your job as mom ever?

What kind of mother/daughter do you want her to be? How did you develop this expectation?

_____
_____
_____
_____
_____

What kind of mother/daughter can she expect you to be? Why? When will this start?

_____
_____
_____
_____
_____

What stifles you from being the best mother/daughter? Why?

_____
_____
_____
_____

ily! (i love you!)

What stops you from forgiving her? Why are still holding that against her?

_____
_____
_____

What stops you from investing in her? Why?

_____
_____
_____
_____

What does your love mean to her?

_____
_____
_____
_____

Why is it hard to meet her expectations?

_____
_____
_____

Does she make her expectations known and clear?
_____
_____
_____
_____
_____
_____

ily! (i love you!)

What would I tell her if I didn't have to worry about getting in trouble or ruining the relationship?

REFLECTION

- What have you learned?
- What will you share about this study with others?
- How will you change based on what you have learned?
- How will you influence/inspire her/others to understand your new behavior/attitude?
- What questions do you still have about her based on this lesson?

_____
_____
_____
_____
_____
_____
_____
_____
_____
_____
_____
_____

ily! (i love you!)

RESOURCES

The Power of a Praying Parent by Stormie Omartian

The Power of a Praying Teen by Stormie Omartian

In Her Own Voice: The Notebook for the Christian Woman by Onedia N. Gage

Love Letters to God from a Teenaged Girl by Onedia N. Gage

Truth

Truth requires honesty. Truth is sabotaged by outside influences – other people, internal psychology and the internet. Truth does not exist in plain sight. Truth now has to be sought and investigated.

You are the nature of each other's truth. You have to be the definition of truth for each other. Once you cannot believe her words to be true, the relationship begins to erode. Let us use the next 30 days to share what has been previously not shared truthfully or when the truth has been omitted. Be the truth. Tell the truth.

What you share can usually be verified on the internet. Do you really want her to find out about you on the internet?

Truth is what really happened. No edits. No omissions. No lying. No changing the facts.

Mother

Your daughter is looking at your life and your lies. She is measuring just how much truth she needs to share based on what you do. When she asks you about incidents or issues, what happens? Do you tell her the truth or just what you think she can handle? What will you do if she finds out the real truth from another source? What happens to your credibility? How will you recover from that loss over something so simple as the truth? The reason we avoid the truth is based on saving our image or avoiding our past. Again, does you image mean more than the truth to your daughter?

As a mother, we define their first truths. At any point, we can be replaced as her authority. We are responsible for not being replaced. Telling the truth maybe challenging because some of your truth is not nice and she may judge you and you are embarrassed. I would rather you tell her a someone else tell her, or again the internet beats you to it.

Truth is your time to be the parent that you wanted to have. Do you remember that feeling when you discovered that your mother had lied to you? As daughters, we were devastated and hurt. Imagine how we make our own daughters feel when we lie or otherwise revise the truth. I thought we included truthfulness in our creed, "the mother I will be" or maybe yours is entitled, "the mother I wished I had."

ily! (i love you!)

Either way, we as mothers made some promises about the mother we would be and that included telling the truth. Although we didn't know how hard it would be, we still promised. As a woman of integrity, we need to keep that promise.

We need to respect our relationship with her and TELL THE WHOLE TRUTH! If you cannot bear for her to ever know, then do not do that activity.

Truth is not a perception. Truth is the uncut, unedited, unadulterated version of the story. The whole story. Truth involves sharing the facts, the feelings resulting from the facts, how the facts were formulated, and how you reached a resolve. You will be free to live without that lie hanging over your head. I promise that you will feel better and you will escape the fear which paralyzes you. Your fear of whether or not she will ever find out and that look or that response will be worse than the actual situation.

Word of caution: you are on borrowed time when you are working to rectify the life and the lies. We are in a race with a powerful tool: the world wide web. The internet is very transparent. Have you ever Googled yourself? You should. Understand the power of the internet and its details so that you understand the impact on your relationship. Reflect on instances which you need to correct and modify and recant. Carefully consider how soon you can rectify the shared information. This will go a long way with your daughter and it will free you from the potential of disaster from lying. A healthy relationship requires truth.

Daughter

Have you ever hidden something from your mother? How did you feel? How hard was it to keep that secret? What happened next? It took years for her to discover you broke her vase, but when she found out she was devastated. Mom's first thought was, 'What else has she lied about?' Your mother is now thinking about all of the details of your interactions. She is then thinking about all of the times that she has trusted you without question. She is second guessing herself about you and her judgment of you. It is essential that you understand how truth impacts a relationship.

Keep in mind truth is what you have defined as the opposite of fake. You owe her the same truth that she wants from you.

What are your lies worth? Do what they cost outweigh what you are trying to avoid? I know that when you lied, it was because you were trying to avoid a particular consequence. Did avoiding that consequence really offer the peace you sought? Is the ultimate consequence worth avoiding the minor one? The long term effect is certainly more severe and certainly outweighs your immediate consequence.

Truth is also about you being true to yourself. Who is that self and what is that truth? Share with her what you like and what you need and what you want as soon as you know. While this is difficult for most, start now understanding you so that you can be whole, healthy and happy. This truth is also understanding the details of yourself. I remember when I was able to say that I loved school. I was thought of as a nerd. I was okay with that because it was about me. I never tried to be someone else – I never hid how I felt about school to impress others. This applies to curfew, grades, virginity and other topics which deal with holding up a false image before others, including your mother.

As mothers, we often have dreams for our children, especially your daughters, and what we want them/her to do. With those desires, she may get carried away. She may be imposing her desires, and even her goals on you. Understand that she wants you to be the best that you can be. So until you can start performing at the best level, expect her guidance, leadership and influence.

Truth is to be shared in love and so that means that you will politely say, "Mom, I have plans. These are what my plans are …" When you share these plans, stay focused on the intent of the words rather than the actual words. Keep in mind that she loves you and wants the best. If your plan does not seem like it will be successful, then expect some feedback because she has lived and has immense experience and only wants the best for you.

ily! (i love you!)

Truth Anecdote

I discovered that my mother had used my social security number when I was 16 years old. I remember when the social security card arrived. I was so excited because there was mail in my name. I did not know what would happen next.

As I am pursing life, I apply for an internship at Allstate Insurance. Along with the application, the company checked my credit history. I was amazed at what happened next: I was questioned about my credit history with a negative tone. I still wonder could I have been denied the internship. I had to explain that those items were not mine. While I explain this, I am enlightened by the fact that this would explain my mother's previous statements and behavior. I was going to college and she insisted that I do not open a checking account and do not apply for any credit cards. I ignored her words.

I am not sure that she ever anticipated me finding out but I am sure that she was unconcerned about the consequences. Truth never shared. Trust destroyed.

I did get the insurance internship. I never looked at her the same. I could no longer appreciate her role.

As a daughter, I was not always truthful. I have lied and omitted information from my mother. However, when I was caught, I confessed, I shared the truth, and realized the she was not ready for the truth.

I am known for my direct communication so I realized that she could not survive my honesty. I am the part of her which she does not want to face. I hold her accountable at a level no other person ever has and ever will. She is not willing to be strong enough to discuss the evil and the wrong. She will not stand up for right when it will leave her without favor.

My truth makes her uncomfortable. It calls her to action.

What does it take to tell the truth? Explain.

_____

_____

_____

_____

What does it take to put your pride aside in order that the truth can be shared?

_____

_____

_____

_____

Why don't you think she can handle the truth? Explain.

_____

_____

_____

_____

Do you like to be lied to? Why do you lie?

_____

_____

_____

ily! (i love you!)

If you are going to have to lie to cover that sin, then why did you do that in the first place?

_____
_____
_____
_____

Why do you feel that she will never find out about you indiscretion? Explain.

_____
_____
_____
_____

Is your lie worth you loss of trust? What will you do to resolve and reconcile that trust? Explain.

_____
_____
_____
_____
_____
_____

What would I tell her if I didn't have to worry about getting in trouble or ruining the relationship?

ily! (i love you!)

REFLECTION

- What have you learned?
- What will you share about this study with others?
- How will you change based on what you have learned?
- How will you influence/inspire her/others to understand your new behavior/attitude?
- What questions do you still have about her based on this lesson?

RESOURCES

Ephesians 4:15

[15] Instead, speaking the truth in love, we will grow to become in every respect the mature body of him who is the head, that is, Christ.

2 Thessalonians 2:10

[10] and all the ways that wickedness deceives those who are perishing. They perish because they refused to love the truth and so be saved.

1 John 1:6-8

[6] If we claim to have fellowship with him and yet walk in the darkness, we lie and do not live out the truth. [7] But if we walk in the light, as he is in the light, we have fellowship with one another, and the blood of Jesus, his Son, purifies us from all[a] sin.

[8] If we claim to be without sin, we deceive ourselves and the truth is not in us.

John 8:32

[32] Then you will know the truth, and the truth will set you free."

2 Corinthians 13:8

[8] For we cannot do anything against the truth, but only for the truth.

ily! (i love you!)

Gage | 82

Consequences of a Great and Poor Relationships

The mother/daughter has many implications. A great relationship means that you have a long lasting relationship and a meaningful relationship. This is also a powerful relationship. The wisdom that a mother offers and the knowledge that a daughter has.

Never expect to be friends with your daughter and mother. You were never designed to be friends. You are to be respectful and supportive of each other. Further, you need to be sure that you take care of your relationship. Most of the time, mothers and daughters have issues when she neglects the relationship. Neglecting this relationship is detrimental to you and your future ability to relate to others. The ability to relate to other women has direct correlation to relating to your mother. Most females who have a difficulty with females have trouble with her mother.

We do not want to sacrifice our relationships with anyone. The mother/daughter relationship helps us remain healthy, happy and whole. When the person that you are related to does not love you or respect you or like you or honor you or value you, it is really hurtful. This feeling causes you to question every one you meet that are designed to love you. Not having this relationship makes you reject others incorrectly. This is your first relationship, daughter, so we need to protect it.

Mother

The matriarch is the female leader of the family. This woman is designed to lead the family. The woman also insures that the family is taught culture, is educated, is taught how to resolve conflict, and is taught family values. As a matriarch, your job is to instruct, lead, teach, and settle. Because we are modern and new age, the definitions of family and motherhood have been revised.

As mothers, we are to teach consequences and we need to remember to respond with the information in mind.

Most mothers will choose to let their children suffer through these consequences. Please carefully consider the consequences on the long term before deciding whether to let them "suffer" and "pay." On certain occasions, we need to punish them personally rather than letting her face the long-term irreversible effects. Keep in mind she is your child and therefore your legacy—what she achieves after you. Please do not try to excuse yourself. At the very least, you are still accountable at all times for what they know and, more importantly, what she does not know. You are responsible for what she does not know. She needs to benefit from your experience. She may not be receptive, she may not appear to be listening, and she may not understand why she needs this information. None of that matters; she needs the information that you have. Do not stop sharing and teaching.

Protect your relationship at all costs. Do not put others and material possessions in front of her. You may explain more of them than you would like about your thought process, behavior, actions and decisions, but you owe it to her to share, especially if you had to learn the hard way. Protect your relationship. It deserves and requires that protection.

Allow no one to hurt her and do not hurt her yourself. Keep focused on her needs. There are severe consequences for neglecting her in all aspects.

Keep your communication open and genuine. You could be replaced as the "source" of information. You are constantly in competition with the internet and her friends so understand that you have what the internet does not: experience and relationship.

Mom, there are consequences for not being mom, consistently and full-time.

Daughter

The Lord says that if you honor you parents then your days on the earth will be long. If you reap what you sow, then you will get back what happens to your mother when you are the mommy.

Consider what the issues really are when you decide to be angry with your mother. You only get one mother. Cherish her. Honor her. Share. Keep her close. Authentically. One of the questions you have been answering is 'what would you tell her if you were not concerned that it would ruin the relationship.' When you consider that question and your answers, be sure to craft that message such that she can receive it and respond to it. Honest but gentle.

Always remember that the same attitude and quick temper you want to use to respond, she may use that same tone, words and attitude. Be careful that you do not get into an argument intending to hurt her by your words, deeds and tone, but rather she hurts you instead; and so much hurt that it feels unrecoverable.

Always remember she is a person with feelings, who is DEEPLY invested in you, who you are and who you will become, and driven to put her best before you. If you hurt her, then you risk sacrifice of a future. Evaluate whether these comments will actually yield the correct results. Mom is a woman too, with similar issues, and is on her own 'last straw.' You may feel justified in your behavior but you really need to reconsider your decision.

Have you ever considered the choices she has made regarding you? She could have given you to foster care, via adoption, relatives, or worse, she could just ignore you while in your presence.

Do you know that she could have done many things other than raise you as her daughter? Do you understand that she could be an embarrassment to you?

Remember to temper your behavior. Ask questions respectfully, humbly. Remember choose remorse when you are shown your wrongdoings.

ily! (i love you!)

Consequences Anecdote

Motherhood is hard. Daughterhood is difficult as well. Our actions have consequences. My mother and father divorced when I was six years old. When she decided to leave him after over a decade of marriage and his physical abuse, I was proud of her. Yes, at six years old, I was proud of her. I knew enough to understand that she had taken a big risk.

When she left, she left me with him. I had no problem with my father but at 6 years old, it meant something when she left me. She did not say goodbye or tell me the plan. By the time she came for me, I really did not want to be bothered with her. She had LEFT me. When I asked her about it, she answered that she thought I would disclose her hiding place. I was crushed. I was already hurt. This impaled our relationship forever. The mutual lack of trust has lasted since that moment.

I outgrew that hurt and have tried repeatedly to build a relationship with her. Nothing has worked.

After that incident, there was the time when I got caught 'skipping school.' I had gone to the doctor. My plan had failed and the school called her at work. When I would not disclose my whereabouts, she told me to pack my clothes and she would take me to my father's house. Upon my arrival, I was content to live with him.

I never felt that she was on my side or would help me. While I have multiple examples of this opinion, we are still not the mother/daughter I always imagined that we would be.

I do not wish that for anyone. Now I do not have either of them, but she is still alive.

The relationship is worth working for.

What are you really losing when you sacrifice your mother/daughter relationship?

_____
_____
_____
_____
_____

What do you really gain from a healthy relationship?

_____
_____
_____
_____
_____

What does it take to reach a healthy relationship? Who do you need to be? Who does she need to be?

_____
_____
_____
_____
_____

ily! (i love you!)

What would I tell her if I didn't have to worry about getting in trouble or ruining the relationship?

REFLECTION

- What have you learned?
- What will you share about this study with others?
- How will you change based on what you have learned?
- How will you influence/inspire her/others to understand your new behavior/attitude?
- What questions do you still have about her based on this lesson?

RESOURCES

Ruth 1:16-18

[16] But Ruth replied, "Don't urge me to leave you or to turn back from you. Where you go I will go, and where you stay I will stay. Your people will be my people and your God my God. [17] Where you die I will die, and there I will be buried. May the LORD deal with me, be it ever so severely, if even death separates you and me." [18] When Naomi realized that Ruth was determined to go with her, she stopped urging her.

Luke 15:11-16

[11] Jesus continued: "There was a man who had two sons. [12] The younger one said to his father, 'Father, give me my share of the estate.' So he divided his property between them.

[13] "Not long after that, the younger son got together all he had, set off for a distant country and there squandered his wealth in wild living. [14] After he had spent everything, there was a severe famine in that whole country, and he began to be in need. [15] So he went and hired himself out to a citizen of that country, who sent him to his fields to feed pigs. [16] He longed to fill his stomach with the pods that the pigs were eating, but no one gave him anything.

Legacy

Legacy—the word and the concept—did not mean anything to me until I had a child. When you have a child, your attitude toward legacy should change—IMMEDIATELY!

As a child, you will appreciate the concept and definition of legacy. When your parents prepare you through your education, maybe provide financial foundation and even give you somewhere to work, with the plan for you to own it all, you will eventually really appreciate who they are and what they do and have done. Only a small percent of parents do any of that; far fewer can do all three.

Legacy is defined as anything handed down from the past, as from an ancestor or predecessor, as defined by Merriam-Webster. Google defines legacy as being given the necessary tools and a head start. Legacy for Gage is the tools needed to pursue a great education and more of it than previously considered great in my family. The courage to dream AND achieve. The ability to move ahead even with a bit of fear. Legacy is the ability to encourage excellence even when others around you question the need.

Legacy is being prepared for the future based on what your parents did in advance. Some of us do not have a legacy. We need to work to create one.

I have created a legacy for my children, but if they do not take it as their own, someone else's kids will have a legacy. I have taught them how important legacy is and we have discussed what to do with the talents and dreams they have.

Mother

Do what you are supposed to do. Do not modify your course. As a high school teacher, I saw children undermine the plans you have for them. However, I ask that you stay focused on your path and do not deter from them.

Mom, be your best self! Remember all that you wanted as a child—wishing for more from your mother. Make sure that you are that mom—even if your child does not seem interested, or does not respond well.

ily! (i love you!)

Remember when we were children, we did not appreciate or understand why certain activities were required. It was only later that you understood that using the correct fork would keep you employed. It was only later that you understood why good grades were important when you graduated without any student loans and was offered automatic acceptance to graduate school.

They do not know what they are going to face. They do not understand what we do. I am a firm believer that we will reap praise and benefit from work when they face what they have been prepared for. We do not even know fully ourselves what they will face. We base our leadership and legacy on what we needed and what we think they will face.

Now to legacy, do not get discouraged if they reject your education and work. Your only job is to do it. Your effectiveness is not measured by their response. Continue to work for what the best is in your life and for your family.

Spend time defining legacy for your family. Keep them focused on the definition of legacy. So much so that they can adopt the philosophy of legacy without too much prompting. They will understand legacy so that they can help with the family accountability. Legacy can easily be disrupted by one loose person. This can help with maintaining the standards within the family. Some families will need to develop their own culture and standards. Create a legacy which completely include who you are.

Be a LEADER! Be an EXAMPLE! That means you keep your moments when you want to quit or your moments which defy the legacy to a minimum and to yourself. You get 30 seconds for a pity party. That is ALL! Pick up the pieces and handle your business!

Daughter

There are many daughters who grow up without a mother, at least not a biological one. There are others who do not have mothers past the age of 18. There are mothers who are overbearing. There are mothers who are inattentive. There are mothers who had the opportunity to raise children but aborted them. There are mothers who are smart, legacy-focused women. Hopefully, your mother is legacy-focused and sharp. Hopefully, you are smart enough to realize her benefits.

If she is overbearing, bossy, and in your business, then she is probably smart and legacy driven. What that means is that she is building a legacy and a life that is based on that legacy. I am hopeful that you recognize her value and worth. All moms are not created equal. All moms do not have the same methods or concerns or beliefs or values.

A legacy will open your future wider than ever. You will be thankful and grateful when your name means something. Many children grow up with nothing and no one. That is unfortunate, however what that means is that we work harder.

A great reputation is better than no reputation or a bad reputation. Time is required to build a powerful reputation. The value of reputation is priceless. Reputation opens closed doors; it adds extra positions which were filled before; it makes opportunity available to you that otherwise was reserved for the inner circle of the leadership.

Your mother's legacy may seem overwhelming and even cumbersome at times. Remember she is paving the way and making particular provisions for you. What would you do without that provision? Her legacy and her name could be a popular judge or the school principal or the teacher. Everyone knows her and they all have an opinion of her. Either way, please understand that she is doing and has done her job.

Yes, her legacy is packed with expectations, some seem impossible. Legacy requires a certain behavior, certain educational levels and particular social groups. This is not too much for you to manage.

Be prepared to be your own legacy. Spread your own legacy. Pass it on to your children and family.

You should use the benefits of the legacy and please do not criticize the concept of legacy. This is an underused family value which usually accompanies success and wealth.

ily! (i love you!)

Legacy Anecdote

As an author, I know my children have issue with my life which creates a legacy for them. I have several other titles as well: teacher, preacher, coach, and advocate. These roles cause people to know me and notice me daily. My daughter asks regularly, even if not out loud, 'Can we please go somewhere one time where people do not stop us to say hello?' I am sympathetic to her but I have lived with the opposite—my mother's name did not mean anything.

Legacy and your name aid in self-worth. The benefit to my daughter will be that she needs someone or something and I cannot physically reach her, then I can send someone to my daughter in her time of distress.

She may never understand the value of my efforts. I will understand if she does not understand. However, my niece experienced my legacy and the value of my name. And quite unexpectedly.

She had moved to Norfolk, Va., married and pregnant, from Houston, Texas. The baby arrived VERY early. I could not travel because I was pregnant as well. As the status of the baby boy progresses, I realize that this is her first child and she may need some support and I need reassurance that _all_ was being done.

I made a phone call to my sorority sister who had the phone number of another sorority sister who worked in the NICU (Neonatal Intensive Care Unit). The nurse introduced herself as 'someone your aunt sent to you.' My niece cried, then called. Thank you was all she could muster.

Later, she spoke about how much better she felt when she had someone who knew her available to her. She felt loved that I sought someone to see after her in my absence.

Legacy has value. Legacy affords privilege.

What do you plan to leave your daughter? What are you hoping Mom will gift you?
_____
_____
_____
_____

What preparations have you made for her post college? What are your plans post college?
_____
_____
_____
_____

Who can/will you call on her behalf to assist her with education or a job?
_____
_____
_____
_____

Have you taught her what she needs to know about the value of legacy?
_____
_____
_____
_____

ily! (i love you!)

Does she know/appreciate who you are and what you do? Do you appreciate who she is?
_____
_____
_____

Why this particular legacy? What are the details of the legacy?
_____
_____
_____

What does your mother do that you can do as well?
_____
_____
_____

What do you want to do with your life where she can open doors for you?
_____
_____
_____

What do you do to contribute to the legacy of your family?
_____
_____

_____

_____

What do you consider your best asset? Your biggest opportunity? Have you shared this with your mother? Did she offer to help or find you a coach to help you with that?

_____

_____

_____

_____

_____

_____

What will you do to extend the legacy she has established for you?

_____

_____

_____

_____

_____

ily! (i love you!)

What would I tell her if I didn't have to worry about getting in trouble or ruining the relationship?

_____
_____
_____
_____
_____
_____
_____
_____
_____
_____
_____
_____
_____
_____
_____
_____
_____

REFLECTION

- What have you learned?
- What will you share about this study with others?
- How will you change based on what you have learned?
- How will you influence/inspire her/others to understand your new behavior/attitude?
- What questions do you still have about her based on this lesson?

_____

_____

_____

_____

_____

_____

_____

_____

_____

_____

_____

_____

ily! (i love you!)

RESOURCES

1 Samuel 1-2

Proverbs 31:10-31 (NIV)

¹⁰ [a]A wife of noble character who can find?
  She is worth far more than rubies.
¹¹ Her husband has full confidence in her
  and lacks nothing of value.
¹² She brings him good, not harm,
  all the days of her life.
¹³ She selects wool and flax
  and works with eager hands.
¹⁴ She is like the merchant ships,
  bringing her food from afar.
¹⁵ She gets up while it is still night;
  she provides food for her family
  and portions for her female servants.
¹⁶ She considers a field and buys it;
  out of her earnings she plants a vineyard.
¹⁷ She sets about her work vigorously;
  her arms are strong for her tasks.
¹⁸ She sees that her trading is profitable,
  and her lamp does not go out at night.
¹⁹ In her hand she holds the distaff
  and grasps the spindle with her fingers.
²⁰ She opens her arms to the poor
  and extends her hands to the needy.
²¹ When it snows, she has no fear for her household;
  for all of them are clothed in scarlet.
²² She makes coverings for her bed;

    she is clothed in fine linen and purple.
23 Her husband is respected at the city gate,
    where he takes his seat among the elders of the land.
24 She makes linen garments and sells them,
    and supplies the merchants with sashes.
25 She is clothed with strength and dignity;
    she can laugh at the days to come.
26 She speaks with wisdom,
    and faithful instruction is on her tongue.
27 She watches over the affairs of her household
    and does not eat the bread of idleness.
28 Her children arise and call her blessed;
    her husband also, and he praises her:
29 "Many women do noble things,
    but you surpass them all."
30 Charm is deceptive, and beauty is fleeting;
    but a woman who fears the LORD is to be praised.
31 Honor her for all that her hands have done,
    and let her works bring her praise at the city gate.

ily! (i love you!)

Technology

Technology for this particular conversation is defined as all media and all visual and any electronic information gathering or transfer. Texting, KIK, Instagram, email and other forms of electronic messaging.

Technology is a great advance in this world. We have made great strides since word of mouth was the only means of sharing information. While we still use word of mouth, it is the most advanced version possible: the internet!

Mother

How are you using the technology at your disposal? Are you still calling her on the phone? Or do you text her when a thought crosses your mind? I am suggesting that you meet her half-way. I am a texter. I am a talker-caller. I do both. She understands that I need to talk at certain times. Otherwise, I am satisfied to text. I also type every single word.

Mom, please make every effort to find what works for your relationship with your daughter. You need to arrive at an understanding of the expectation of communication via technology. As you text, please be sure to ask for a translation of what you do not understand.

Lastly, mom, I am a proponent of checking the contents of her cell phone (as long as she is a teenager, you should consider this practice), email, and other communication avenues. Yes, you may be a little disappointed by what you find but you also may be afforded the opportunity to intervene at some critical instances. The ability to save your child's life or intercept the messages of a child predator or the unwanted advances of a school boy or the bullying that may be happening is the best thing to happen for your child. She <u>needs</u> you to be a STRONG woman for her. This is NOT a popularity award seeking role. You are her MOTHER. Nobody else is assigned as replacement or backup. And you do not get an assistant. Be her MOTHER. She only gets one and you are hers!

ily! (i love you!)

Daughter

You are texting 40 characters each minute. That is not even your top speed. Keep in mind you and your mother learned to text nearly at the same time. Texting was not initially on every cell phone. You will have to translate from time to time. Mommy does not know all of those terms and abbreviations.

Further, remember that she will always love to hear the sound of your voice. Remember that she loves you and hopes that you know what that means. You are her life's work. You are the beneficiary to all of her hard work. You are able to access all types of areas of her being that others will NEVER access. Not even your male siblings carry the same weight as you do. Please do not take advantage of the situation and please do not hut her—intentionally nor unintentionally.

Be wise with your use of technology. Everyone that wants to 'follow' or 'friend' you is not your friend or someone who means you well. If something about that interaction does not feel right, please let your mother know and inform the police.

Lastly, your mother's intentions to protect you are genuine. Please understand that she wants the best for you. Please do not take nude selfies nor share them with anyone. First of all, the recipient could share them with others which would bring you immense pain. You do not believe he would do that, but he might. The other detail is to remember that if someone else got his phone, they could share your photos. What would either of you be able to do about that? It would be unfortunate but there is nothing that could be done.

A few years ago, this happened to a young lady and as a result, her photos were found on a pornographic website. She was featured on Dateline. She cried almost the entire interview. She quit going to public school her senior year and was home schooled until graduation. She was devastated. She never thought it was possible that it would happen to her.

Secondly, the photos you take are backed up in case of loss of phone or data, etc. That photo is somewhere in cyberspace—the cloud. Do you really want to take that chance?

Your future could be damaged by 'one little harmless selfie.'

Lastly, how would you feel if a photo of your mother was somewhere on the internet? What if that child is yours on the internet naked? What if your child finds you on the internet naked?

Please consider all of those details as you consider taking naked selfies.

If he needs a naked selfie, then he needs to put a ring on it.

ily! (i love you!)

Technology Anecdote

The name of this book came out of a Mother Daughter workshop. I was discussing that message abbreviations. After much conversation, one mother asked what does 'ily' mean. The daughter then responded frantically, 'I love you.'

I asked the daughter if she thought that she did not love her because Mom had not responded. The daughter said yes.

I went on to explain that is why we ask for the translation and that is why we share the translation as soon as possible.

Technology communication is very important. Both parties are responsible.

I believe that outburst and revelation was good for all parties.

When I see something new with my daughter, I ask. I still spell everything out so sometimes she accommodates me by spelling the words out, too.

Why are you afraid of and avoid looking through her phone?

_____
_____
_____
_____

What do you do to protect her from internet issues? Her internet safety?

_____
_____
_____
_____

How much do you reveal about your fears regarding her technology use?

_____
_____
_____
_____

What do you want her to know that you have been previously unable to discuss?

_____
_____
_____

ily! (i love you!)

What are you trying to hide from her?
_____
_____
_____
_____

What do you think she is hiding from you?
_____
_____
_____
_____

When do you intend to delete the inappropriate pictures, messages, and objects from your electronic devices?
_____
_____
_____
_____

What would I tell her if I didn't have to worry about getting in trouble or ruining the relationship?

ily! (i love you!)

REFLECTION

- What have you learned?
- What will you share about this study with others?
- How will you change based on what you have learned?
- How will you influence/inspire her/others to understand your new behavior/attitude?
- What questions do you still have about her based on this lesson?

_____
_____
_____
_____
_____
_____
_____
_____
_____
_____

RESOURCES

http://www.bbc.com/news/technology-26121434

http://theconversation.com/the-dangers-of-kids-using-technology-a-modern-day-horror-story-we-like-to-tell-27151

ily! (i love you!)

Gage | 112

Quality Time

My love language is quality time. I believe that quality time is the best thing for me in any relationship. I just want to figure out how to spend time together. I may just want to be in the presence of the person. This could apply to my husband, my friends and my children.

When my daughter and I are together, I do not always have to talk. She sits next to me and we sleep or watch a movie or read. It is an amazing moment when this happens. Neither of us is uncomfortable by that silence. We can just sit there. There are the quite the opposite times when we talk non-stop.

Quality time is defined by each of you—no one person's definition is correct alone. The method by which we spend time together is a compromise and flexible based today's needs. Each experience will be unique. I crave time to spend with my daughter. And with any relationship, sometimes there are differences of schedules when time has to be measured in communication. This is critical for everyone to define time and schedule accordingly.

Keep your word. When you say you will spend time together, do everything in your power to be there, on time and present in the moment.

Being there means that you are there with one another. In the same space at the same time engaging one another. This is not time for one more phone call or one more email or one more text. Be one time—not late—early. Start your activity on time. Being on time is a sign of respect of each other. Being on time says that this is important to me.

Engaging one another means that you are active within the activity. This means all electronics down and all attention is on the other person. You are actively listening and you are attentive. Depending on the length of time, there may be an appropriate time for a break, but really consider doesn't she deserve uninterrupted time—however much time is available? Yes, she deserves your uninterrupted time and your undivided attention.

These actions speak volumes to the importance of her and your relationship with her.

ily! (i love you!)

In the Love Language test, quality time is one of the languages. I want you to consider that in order for a couple of the others to work, you have to be in each other's presence, which may be defined as quality time. Physical touch requires presence. While words of affirmation and giving gifts do not require your presence, it goes along way when you are present.

I would encourage you to seek your best efforts in order to spend the best amount to time that you can with her so that she can knows you love and care for her. This is important. This relationship shapes so many others. Please use your earthly time wisely—it is not guaranteed from day to day. You do not get to pick when you die. You will regret when she is gone and you can admit that you did not give your very best to her. Lastly, remember you cannot be replaced but you can have your time rerouted to someone or something else. Consistent rejection will cause you to choose to spend her time in other ways and with other people. Choose carefully. This is a huge ship, which requires time to turn around.

Mother

Make time for her. Get to know her. Ask questions. I have included some samples in the appendix. You are her guide. She needs your leadership: DAILY. You need to realize that she needs your voice, your guidance, and your love. Don't make her find out the important stuff from a man that you do not know or like (a temporary source also known as the boyfriend) or her friends (whom you also do not know) or worse than the previously mentioned sources combined—the internet.

Be there! You do not have a substitute or back up. Be there! You have 18 short years which seem like they will never end, but if not done properly, you may spend the next 18 trying to recover, rectify and recuperate from this relationship.

What does she think is more important than she is? What do you spend most of your waking moments doing? What happens when she wants your time, attention, advice, and/or opinion? What does she think will happen when she interrupts you? Does she feel that you will listen to her when she needs you to her?

These are questions you need to consider. Her perception is her reality which means it is REAL. This is what she knows, feels, sees and shares. She repeats this to her friends. They compare notes, and based on that comparison, you are graded or judged. Are you the best Mom you can be? Without excuses or condition, are you the best Mom you can be? What does it take for you to be the best Mom? How long before you can implement the plan? If you are brave, ask her what would that be? What is required to be a better mother to you?

Daughter

Stop texting while she is talking to you! She has told you one hundred times that it is rude to text while she is talking. However, this is deeper than disrespect. Your texting communicates that someone is more important to you. You are no longer demonstrating how important she is the way you used to. She is not the star in your movie. She is after everyone and everything. You may feel the same way but she also suffers with the thought of where did the time go.

Please forgive us for working and achieving and striving. We had aspirations for our lives when we were your age and we are trying to see them to fruition. You were the second element on that list: 1) husband, 2) daughter, 3) thriving career, and, 4) great social life. 99% of all women could agree that our lists are similar in content and order, so understand we are working to achieve a legacy for you. While that does not justify some of the important events and moments we have missed, we certainly want you to understand that the decision we made to miss your event was weighed heavily against what the other situation was. This is the valuable lesson of choices.

Sometimes it is between miss this meeting where she will make the commission we will use for the family's vacation or go to the awards banquet. When the meeting's four hours pays for a week in Disney World, she had to sacrifice the awards banquet. She compared both possible disappointments: the awards ceremony versus no vacation. She could not do both this time, so she provided the vacation. You may have never been privy to that depth of information but those are the decisions we make. Some of which we may never disclose to you. Some we may share later. Become a household partner by understanding when situations happen. Ask respectfully for clarity when you need to understand. Also understand when she says that she cannot share.

Quality time is important to the health of your relationship. Find a way to spend time with her and enjoy it. Open up to her and share what you think about, life choices you have made, and the future you have planned for yourself. Become the best daughter in the best mother and daughter team ever.

Be the daughter she can be proud of as well. Make it a regular time to spend with her.

ily! (i love you!)

What does she think is more important than she is? What do you spend most of your waking moments doing? What happens when she wants your time, attention, advice, and/or opinion? What does she think will happen when she interrupts you? Does she feel that you will listen to her when she needs you to her?

These are questions you need to consider. Her perception is her reality which means it is REAL. This is what she knows, feels, sees and shares. She repeats this to her friends. They compare notes, based on that comparison you are graded or judged. Are you the best daughter you can be? Without excuses or condition, are you the best daughter you can be? What does it take for you to be the best daughter? How long before you can implement the plan? If you are brave, ask her what would that be? What is required to be a better daughter to you?

Set an appointment! I have included a list of suggested activities in case you need some assistance with ideas.

Quality Time Anecdote

I spend time with my daughter and we do each other's favorite things when we are together. We have some things in common and for the areas we do not have in common we share with each other. From time to time, we do something we have never done.

WE determine what we do by our mood. Our time is uninterrupted and we have each other's undivided attention.

We come back from that event on our time together refreshed, renewed and closer. We need time to talk when there's no one else around, so we can both speak freely and so that we can discuss great solutions for our issues or victories.

When my daughter realized that I could play basketball, she was completely surprised and excited. She thinks it is cool that I know about and can play her favorite sport. This deepened our relationship.

I use this time to share my heart and my fears.

I love our time together. I believe that she does too.

It should be time that you cherish and enjoy. It is a time to love and teach.

ily! (i love you!)

What does she think is more important than she is?

_____
_____
_____
_____

What do you spend most of your waking moments doing?

_____
_____
_____
_____

What happens when she wants your time, attention, advice, and/or opinion?

_____
_____
_____
_____

What does she think will happen when she interrupts you?

_____
_____
_____

Does she feel that you will listen to her when she needs you to her?

_____
_____
_____
_____

Are you the best mom/daughter you can be? Without excuses or condition, are you the best mom/daughter you can be?

_____
_____
_____
_____

What does it take for you to be the best mom/daughter?

_____
_____
_____
_____

How long before you can implement the plan?

_____
_____

ily! (i love you!)

_____

_____

If you are brave, ask her what would that be?

_____

_____

_____

_____

What is required to be a better mother/daughter to you?

_____

_____

_____

_____

What would I tell her if I didn't have to worry about getting in trouble or ruining the relationship?

_____
_____
_____
_____
_____
_____
_____
_____
_____
_____
_____
_____
_____
_____
_____
_____
_____

ily! (i love you!)

REFLECTION

- What have you learned?
- What will you share about this study with others?
- How will you change based on what you have learned?
- How will you influence/inspire her/others to understand your new behavior/attitude?
- What questions do you still have about her based on this lesson?

_____
_____
_____
_____
_____
_____
_____
_____
_____
_____
_____

RESOURCES

Ruth 1:15-18

[15] "Look," said Naomi, "your sister-in-law is going back to her people and her gods. Go back with her."

[16] But Ruth replied, "Don't urge me to leave you or to turn back from you. Where you go I will go, and where you stay I will stay. Your people will be my people and your God my God. [17] Where you die I will die, and there I will be buried. May the LORD deal with me, be it ever so severely, if even death separates you and me." [18] When Naomi realized that Ruth was determined to go with her, she stopped urging her.

Acts 9:4-9

[4] He fell to the ground and heard a voice say to him, "Saul, Saul, why do you persecute me?"

[5] "Who are you, Lord?" Saul asked.

"I am Jesus, whom you are persecuting," he replied. [6] "Now get up and go into the city, and you will be told what you must do."

[7] The men traveling with Saul stood there speechless; they heard the sound but did not see anyone. [8] Saul got up from the ground, but when he opened his eyes he could see nothing. So they led him by the hand into Damascus. [9] For three days he was blind, and did not eat or drink anything.

ily! (i love you!)

Gage | 124

Transparency

Transparency is difficult to manage. Transparency combines communication and honesty and trust.

Being transparent means that when she asks you what is wrong, you can respond with the truth. You can stop saying nothing which is a lie. There's plenty to talk about but you do not trust her with the response that you would like but expect something else altogether. Transparency needs to be evident in your relationship. The biggest question is how to have this transparency and not ruin what we have in a relationship. The question we have been answering for nine chapters, "What would you tell her if you would not risk the relationship?"

This question is designed to help you develop a practice of transparency. The first practice for transparency is understanding how to communicate so that the transparency is not a shock to yourself. Secondly, that writing is to practice how to share that information. When you see your words in writing, it helps you to organize how that will come out exactly. You will want to rearrange or share in a different order that which needs to be shared.

When we are transparent, we do not want to confuse that with mean, unloving, rude nor disrespectful. This is not what we are striving for when you are being transparent. The first objective is to reveal your heart. You are also revealing your mind and your intentions.

You are trying to enhance the relationship not ruin it when you are being transparent. Everyone will define and approach this differently, however please understand transparency should also build trust. It is being able to say what you should have said long ago but did not have the courage.

Mother

Share the family secrets. This is the best start. Many families have secrets but they are not revealed until something tragic happens and the damage is immeasurable. The damage is horrific; often unrecoverable.

ily! (i love you!)

This will be so detrimental, recovery appears impossible. Imagine finding other family members on social media.

Share the family health history. Many of us go to the doctor and we are ignorant to the family health history which makes it harder to be helped at the doctor's office.

Please share so that when your health history is disclosed, we are not surprised or in disbelief. Please share. It is unfair to not share.

Finally, let us understand how to share our feelings. Most children do not know how to respond to affection and compliments. All people need affirmation and uplift. This is the time to share. Make sure she knows her sense of worth. This serves two purposes: She knows how special she is so when someone tells her what she is not then she can dismiss that rather than consider it as truth. The second reason is that the first time she hears something great about herself is from you rather than someone else. She does not have to compare or question if she hears her positive worth from you.

Self-esteem is healthy and high when nurtured and stimulated. Otherwise, it is on a roller coaster that it is often difficult to recover from. Please find a way to affirm your daughter so that she does not have to live on the conditional words of others. When others speak to her, she needs to have a companion between you, her true voice and the stranger.

Reveal your heart to her!

Daughter

It is time to ask all of your questions. It is time to share all of your needs and all of your thoughts to your mother. For the first time, use her as your complete source, instead of Google or your friends. Yes, she is going to be overwhelmed and surprised and she may even be speechless, however you need to share. You need to share with her what you need to know.

As a daughter, you need to help her to be your mother. When she asks about what is wrong, answer her—honestly and accurately. She deserves it and she needs it.

She is interested in your life. She wants the best for you. She wants the dreams she has for you to come true. She wants the dreams you have for yourself to come true. She wants you to have those without very much drama, if any. She wants you to not have much trouble. She wants you to learn from her mistakes. Your mistakes are not unavoidable but they could be limited, which is the goal.

Finally, daughters, we need to consider the reason God matched us up with our mothers. What do I need to learn from her? What is this designed to show me? What will I see with her? What does she do to insure that I am ready for the world? How will I grow as a girl and daughter because I am her daughter? Is she the great example that I need to be great as well? Do I follow her and respect her as I should? Share with your mother what she needs to be your mother!

ily! (i love you!)

Transparency Anecdote

As a high school teacher, hundreds of girls cross my path each year that I impact in one way or another. Most often, I do not know my full impact on their lives. I have recently been exposed to know more about my impact on them, the trust they have in me and the respect they have for me.

Several young ladies have asked questions of me that they cannot ask their mothers. They ask me about boys, college, careers, and even sex. These topics and questions are not unique to anyone. These are common topics and they will never stop being asked. As a daughter, mother, mentor and coach, I am careful how I answer those questions because I have been awarded the trusted advisor. I have also been considered a non-judger. I am trusted. I am believed. I am respected. I am loved. I am a role model. I am a mentor. When I am sharing my opinion and my advice, I am conscious of the fact my opinion is being used and it is possibly being shared with others who do not know me well.

I was chosen to offer my opinion, facts and experience. These experiences taught me as a mother, to start the dialogue about boys, college, career and sex early. This conversation was uncomfortable for my daughter but I felt confident that the discussion was important and would be life-changing. My initiative removed the mystery of those topics along with my opinion being offered first. I closed the door on whether or not I could talk about it and whether or not she was ready. I affirmed her and helped her understand the next stages of her life.

I resolved that I would not let her friends or the internet win over my parenting.

I was transparent first. I am honest. I wait for her to process the information I have shared and I ask her if she has any questions. I listen if she does and I want for her to think of those questions. I encourage her to ask her friend's questions as well.

I encourage moms to talk about what other daughters are sharing, so that this collective discussion and bring a better daughter to each of us.

What are you hiding/keeping from her and are hoping she never finds out?

_____
_____
_____
_____

What do you need to be more transparent?

_____
_____
_____
_____

What do you need to do so that she feels that she can be more transparent with you?

_____
_____
_____
_____

What are you afraid to talk to her about? Why?

_____
_____
_____

ily! (i love you!)

What should be sharing but are not?

_____
_____
_____

What are you hoping she brings up first?

_____
_____
_____
_____

What does it take to be honest with her?

_____
_____
_____
_____

Do you respect her? Why or why not? Does she know that?

_____
_____
_____
_____

Do you trust her? Why or why not? Does she know that?

_____
_____
_____
_____

Do you ever question her integrity? Why or why not? Does she know that? Did you ever share that with her? Did that situation improve?

_____
_____
_____
_____

ily! (i love you!)

What would I tell her if I didn't have to worry about getting in trouble or ruining the relationship?

REFLECTION

- What have you learned?
- What will you share about this study with others?
- How will you change based on what you have learned?
- How will you influence/inspire her/others to understand your new behavior/attitude?
- What questions do you still have about her based on this lesson?

_____
_____
_____
_____
_____
_____
_____
_____
_____
_____
_____

ily! (i love you!)

RESOURCES

Job 12:22

²² He reveals the deep things of darkness
    and brings utter darkness into the light.

Esther 2:10

¹⁰ Esther had not revealed her nationality and family background, because Mordecai had forbidden her to do so.

Daniel 2:22

²² He reveals deep and hidden things;
    he knows what lies in darkness,
    and light dwells with him.

Luke 2:35

³⁵ so that the thoughts of many hearts will be revealed. And a sword will pierce your own soul too."

ily!

This all started because of a class I facilitated and one mother daughter team came to a realization that they had a communication gap. In this session, they are realized that they needed to share more and translate and ask more questions. They reached an understanding which I hope is lasting and meaningful.

This book is necessary because it will help both of you. You have grown in this short period of time. You should realize that you directly affect each other. From moodiness to mistakes, everything you do affects her. Please remember that whatever you do has a life-long effect, either publicly or/and privately.

Be aware of the words that you speak. Those also have a lasting effect. At just the moment when we want to become the mayor or the governor or some other political figure, we need to feel confident that we can hear with the authoritative voice of mother saying, 'Yes, you can.' Likewise, you do not want to prove your lack of love for her by rejecting her verbally. Both of you could do some serious damage.

Pray for her. For both of you. She needs you to pray for her. These prayers are powerful and lasting. When she prays for you, God has the opportunity to change her heart which she is asking Him to change yours.

If you are really serious about the health of the relationship and your relationship with God, then pray together! Prayer has the power to change all things.

Pray with a zeal and fervency that the Lord will heal and forgive, love and keep, nurture and create. You are on a journey with each other. She should not want to quit and you should not make her want to quit.

Send ily! as often as you think of her, even if you are mad. Say I love you every time you speak or write her because you do love her and she needs to know it, in all of the possible ways.

As a mother and daughter, I have revealed my heart to you in hopes that you will measure your relationship with gold and cherish it intentionally and on purpose.

Forgive her for EVERYTHING!!!!!

LOVE her unconditionally!

ily! (i love you!)

What would you tell her that will inspire, enhance, encourage and rejuvenate your relationship?
_____
_____
_____
_____

Do you feel differently about her now?
_____
_____
_____
_____

What will you do with this new information?
_____
_____
_____
_____

How can you be a better mother/daughter now that you are more equipped before?
_____
_____
_____

What would I tell her if I didn't have to worry about getting in trouble or ruining the relationship?

_____
_____
_____
_____
_____
_____
_____
_____
_____
_____
_____
_____
_____
_____
_____
_____

ily! (i love you!)

REFLECTION

- What have you learned?
- What will you share about this study with others?
- How will you change based on what you have learned?
- How will you influence/inspire her/others to understand your new behavior/attitude?
- What questions do you still have about her based on this lesson?

_____
_____
_____
_____
_____
_____
_____
_____
_____
_____

Appendix

1. Blank calendars (12)
2. Ideas for activities
3. All About Me Quiz
4. Suggested Questions
5. Conflict Resolution
6. Goals Worksheets
7. Mission
8. Vision
9. Values
10. Dreams
11. Resources
    a. Websites
    b. Books

ily! (i love you!)

Calendar Pages

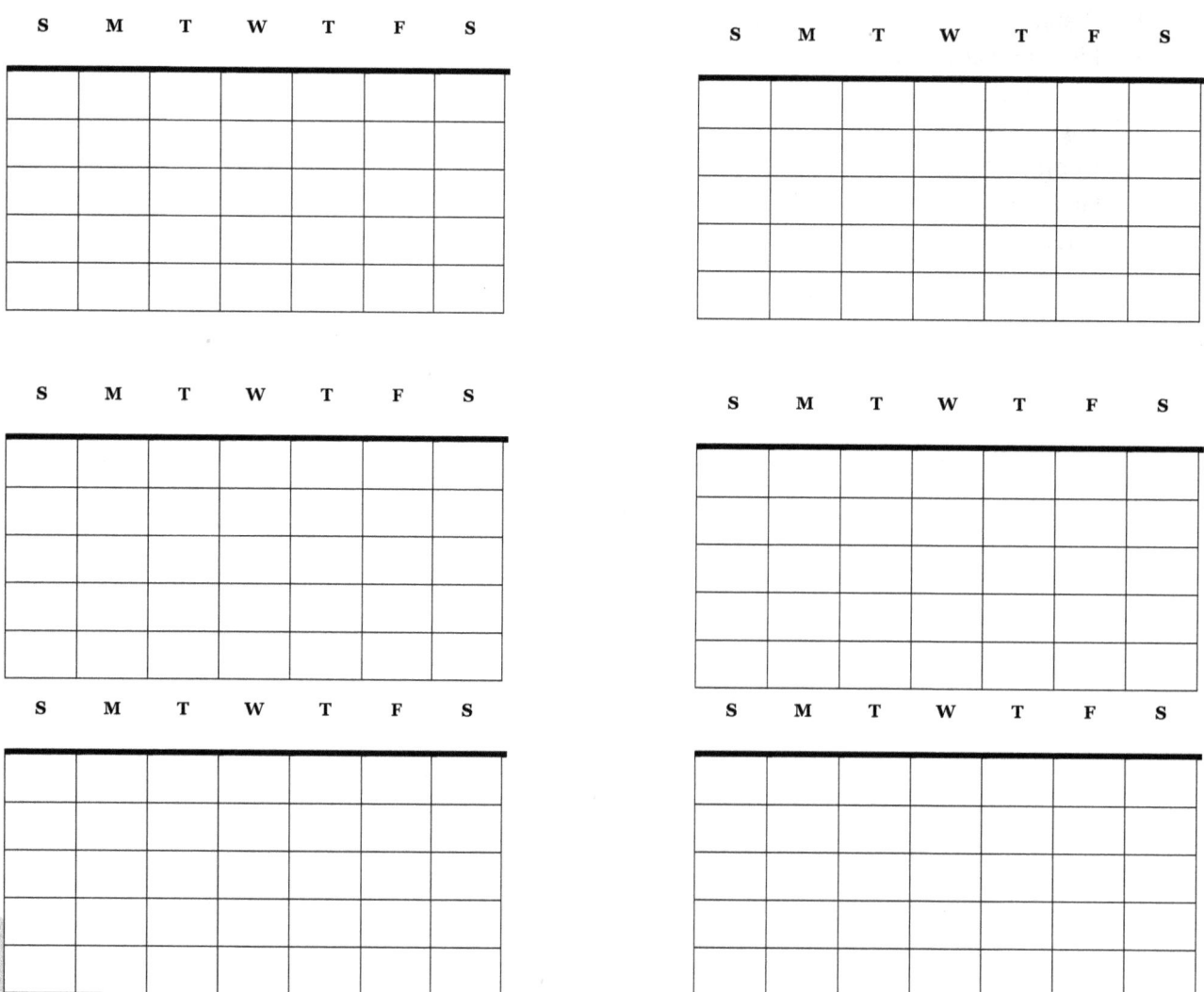

Gage | 140

A Mother Daughter Relationship Workbook

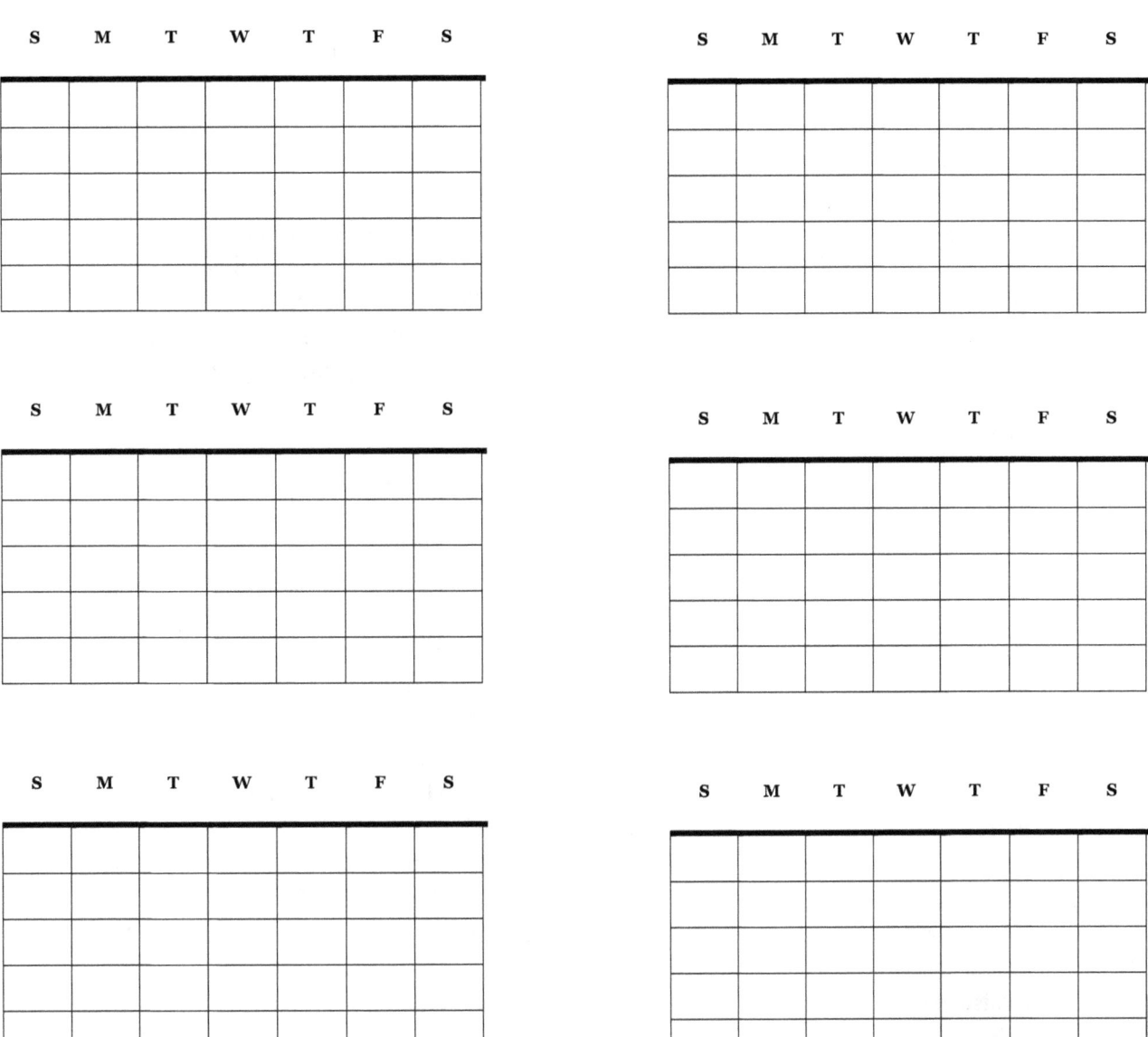

ily! (i love you!)

Activity Ideas

1. Movie night
2. Zoo
3. Fishing
4. Make-up Experiments
5. Hair Experiments
6. Museum
7. Lunch
8. Brunch
9. Shopping
10. Workshops
11. Spa Visits
12. Video games
13. Letter writing
14. Texting
15. Phone calls
16. Dinner
17. Sports
18. Driving
19. Paintball
20. Go cart racing
21. Horseback riding
22. Painting
23. Exercise class
24. Reading
25. Skydiving
26. Swim with the Sharks
27. Swim with the \Dolphins
28. Roller Coasters
29. Volunteering
30. Start a business together
31. Ski
32. Vacation
33. Prayer
34. Church
35. School
36. Sculpting class
37. Pottery class
38. Women's Conference
39. Quilting
40. Walking
41. Biking
42. Historic Home Tours
43. Trolley Rides
44. Bible Study
45. Stage Plays
46. Musicals
47. Build a volcano
48. Build a snowman
49. Jet skiing
50. Cooking

All About Me Quiz

1. What 5 of my favorite movies?
2. What is my ideal meal?
3. Where is my favorite place to read?
4. What are my favorite book titles?
5. Who are my favorite authors?
6. What is my dream vacation?
7. What is my favorite color?
8. What is my favorite time of day
9. What do I do to escape?
10. Where do I go to escape?
11. What is my favorite time of day?
12. What is my favorite time of year?
13. What do I do to relax?
14. What is my favorite type of music?
15. Who is my favorite musician(s)?
16. What is my favorite dessert?
17. What is my favorite drink?
18. What is my favorite musical instrument?
19. What are the instruments that I want to learn to play?
20. What makes me cry?
21. What makes me laugh?
22. What do I do for fun?
23. What inspires me?
24. What are 5 things I want to achieve?
25. What is my favorite snack?
26. What is my favorite sport?
27. What is my favorite poem?
28. What is my favorite poet?
29. Who do I call when it's going well?

ily! (i love you!)

30. Who do I call when it is not going well?
31. Where do I want to travel?
32. What is my favorite flavor of ice cream?
33. What is my favorite brand of ice cream?
34. What do I do for exercise?
35. What is my pet peeve?
36. What is my favorite television show?
37. Why do I like those movies?
38. Why do I like this show?
39. What shuts me down?
40. What do I fear?
41. What makes me happy?
42. What makes me smile?
43. What do I need?
44. What are my strengths?
45. What are my weaknesses?
46. What is my favorite car?
47. What is my favorite car color?
48. What is my favorite restaurant?
49. What is my favorite store?
50. What is my favorite pet?
51. What is my ideal profession?
52. What does my mother think I should be?
53. What does it take for my love tank to be full?
54. What do I do when I am sad?
55. What do I do when I am happy?
56. Who would I like to meet and spend time with (public and famous)?
57. How do you know when I am happy?
58. Why are birthdays so important to me?
59. What do I dream of?
60. What is my definition of success?

Suggested Questions

1. What would you like your mother to know right now?
2. What would you like your daughter to do right now?
3. What are your dreams for your daughter?
4. What are your dreams for your mother?
5. What is your role as mother?
6. What is your role as daughter?
7. What do you wish you had in common with your mother?
8. What did you have in common with your daughter at this age?
9. What is your favorite detail about your daughter?
10. What is your favorite detail about your mother?
11. What do you wish your daughter would do more of?
12. What do you wish your mother would do better or more of?
13. What are your personal goals?
14. How can you communicate better with your daughter?
15. How can you communicate better with your mother?
16. What are your goals for your daughter?

ily! (i love you!)

Plan for Conflict Resolution

When we have conflict, we will do the following:

- Remain calm
- Be honest
- Listen completely
- Be fair
- Don't interrupt the other person while she is speaking
- Remember we love each other
- Remember not to be critical
- Do not judge

Goal Worksheets

What are your goals for yourself? One year? Three years? Five years? 10 years?

_____

_____

_____

_____

_____

_____

What are your goals for her?

_____

_____

_____

What are you afraid of trying?

_____

_____

_____

ily! (i love you!)

What are you afraid of achieving?
_____
_____
_____

What does it take to overcome your fears?
_____
_____
_____

How can you help her overcome her fears?
_____
_____
_____

How can you share your fears with her? Are you afraid of her reaction?
_____
_____
_____

Mission

What is your mission in life? Your Personal Mission Statement.

_____
_____
_____
_____
_____
_____
_____
_____
_____
_____
_____
_____
_____
_____
_____

ily! (i love you!)

Vision

What is your vision for yourself? Your personal vision statement.

_____
_____
_____
_____
_____
_____
_____
_____
_____
_____
_____
_____
_____
_____

Values

What are your values? What do you value?

_____
_____
_____
_____
_____
_____
_____

How did you develop those values and that value system?

_____
_____
_____
_____
_____
_____
_____

ily! (i love you!)

Dreams

What are your dreams? What does it take to achieve those dreams?

Resources

Dr. Gary Chapman   The Five Love Languages for Teens

Dr. Gary Chapman   The Five Love Languages

Sam McBuatney   Guess How Much I Love You

ily! (i love you!)

Gage | 154

Acknowledgements

God, thank You for Your plans for me. Thank You for *ily! (I love you!) Mother Daughter Relationship Workbook* and choosing me to complete Your project. I just want to please You. Thank You for continuing to anoint me and to invest in me and my gifts, which keep surprising me. Thank You for loving and forgiving me.

Hillary and Nehemiah, thank you for supporting me and my endeavors. Thank you for loving me, especially when I do nothing without a pen and a clipboard, thank you for enduring my late nights, your ideas, the sounding board, the love and the support. Thank you for celebrating our legacy.

Mr. Patrick W. Bell, well there are many words I would like to utter but for now, however, thank you seems most appropriate at this time!

Kimberly 'Ann' Joiner, thank you for reading and offering me feedback for the one of the hardest I have ever written. Thank you for sharing your gifts with me. Always keep your relationship with your mother powerful and awesome! Start out great with Madison and you will never have to wish you had!

To my prayer partners and to my accountability partners, thank you for the long talks and the powerful prayers and the encouragement.

To the women and daughters who this will reach and empower and touch and affect, may these words empower you and help you fervently seek God and reach some resolve. May you be inspired to achieve your goals and dreams. May you enhance your relationship with God so that your other relationships will also improve. May you enhance your self-esteem through prayer and studying. May you have courage and peace. Share love the best you can until you can share love without reservation.

ily! (i love you!)

A Mother Daughter Relationship Workbook

About the Mother/Daughter

The Mother/Daughter is passionate about the relationships of mothers and daughters. She is doing everything in her power to ensure that she and her daughter have the ultimate healthy relationship. She and her biological mother do not have a relationship. She does not want to pass on such a raggedy legacy.

She has since adopted a mother who nurtures her and chastises her as required.

You may invite her to coach, facilitate a mother/daughter workshop in your church, organizations and family. You can reach her at onediagage@onediagage.com, @onediagage, www.onediagage.com, facebook.com/onediagage, youtube.com/onediagage, blogtalkradio.com/onediagage.

www.mymotherdaughter.com

ily! (i love you!)

PREACHER ♦ PRAYER WARRIOR ♦ TEACHER ♦ SMALL GROUP LEADER

To invite Rev. Gage to preach, teach, and pray, Please contact us at

@onediangage (twitter) ♦ onediagage@onediagage.com ♦ facebook.com/onediagage

youtube.com/onediagage ♦ blogtalkradio.com/onediagage ♦ www.onediagage.com

www.mymotherdaughter.com

ily! (i love you!)

A Mother Daughter Relationship Workbook

Publishing

Do you have a book you want to write, but do not know what to do?

Do you have a book you need to publish but do not know how to start?

Would publishing move your career forward?

Let us help

onediagage@purpleink.net ♦ www.purpleink.net

713.705.5530 or 512.715.4243

www.ingramcontent.com/pod-product-compliance
Lightning Source LLC
Chambersburg PA
CBHW080546170426
43195CB00016B/2699